THE
ART OF
DISAGREEING

———————————

HOW TO
KEEP CALM
AND STAY
FRIENDS
IN HARD
CONVERSATIONS

———————————

GAVIN
ORTLUND

thegoodbook
COMPANY

The Art of Disagreeing
© Gavin Ortlund, 2025

Published by:
The Good Book Company

thegoodbook.com | thegoodbook.co.uk
thegoodbook.com.au | thegoodbook.co.nz | thegoodbook.co.in

Published in association with the literacy agency of Wolgemuth & Wilson.

Cover design by Faceout Studio | Design and art direction by André Parker

ISBN: 9781802541403 | JOB-007978 | Printed in India

For Abigail
The universe would be incomplete without her

CONTENTS

Why Disagreement Is Difficult

I read recently that political disagreements are making Thanksgiving dinners shorter.[1] When those in attendance supported different political parties, the meals were 30 to 50 minutes briefer.[2] What a poignant reflection on modern society. We can't even be around each other as much!

Perhaps there are other factors involved in our shrinking Thanksgiving meals. Even so, I suspect most of us recognize that in the modern world, we are losing the ability to disagree well. Whether it's about politics or religion or the culture wars or more trivial things, it's hard to deny the temperature has dramatically risen.

---

1 I use this illustration at the risk of offending my non-American readers right out of the gate—just substitute another holiday meal to relate better to the point!

2 M. Keith Chen and Ryne Rohla, "The Effect of Partisanship and Political Advertising on Close Family Ties," www.science.org/doi/10.1126/science.aaq1433?mod=article_inline (accessed May 29, 2024). Thanks to Sam Allberry for drawing my attention to this article.

Increasingly the assumption seems to be that people on the other side are not simply wrong but *evil*. Or, at the very least, we feel that we must "win" on each point of disagreement, lest evil prevail. Social media and cable news are polarizing us, and it's not good.

Many of us can probably relate to this phenomenon at a personal level. We have lost friendships because of heated disagreements. We have coworkers we steer clear of in the parking lot or fellow church members we avoid after the service. We have family members with whom we cannot speak about certain subjects—or perhaps we cannot speak to them at all.

If that is you, this book is not here to scold or inhibit you. I hope that by the time you finish it, you will feel empowered and hopeful—like you have been given "a second wind" for how to approach disagreements in your life. I hope it reduces guilt and pressure, and gives you a sense of freedom and confidence to move forward.

The Art of Healthy Disagreement

The first step is to recognize that disagreement *itself* is not the problem.

Years ago I recall the late pastor and author Tim Keller interacting with critical responses to one of his books. Instead of noting areas of disagreement, he had a section in his responses called "intriguing."[3] What a wonderful way to categorize our disagreements!

---

3 Timothy Keller, *Shaped by the Gospel: Doing Balanced, Gospel-Centered Ministry in Your City* (Zondervan, 2016), p. 94-98.

Without disagreement, life would be boring. Disagreement is where we discover opportunities for learning, freshness, new beginnings. Someone once said that you get married for your similarities, but you stay married for your differences.

The Inklings (the literary group to which C.S. Lewis and J.R.R. Tolkien belonged) often had disagreements. According to George Watson, Lewis *valued* them—so much so that he prolonged them:

> *"He did not even share the views of friends like Tolkien in matters concerning literature or religion, or not always ... but then agreement would have spoiled the game, and Lewis in debate tried to keep disagreement going for as long as he reasonably could, and sometimes longer. If I were ever to be asked what I learned from him, that would be my reply: the art of disagreement."* [4]

I like that little line: "agreement would have spoiled the game." I picture Lewis there at the pub. Discussion has revealed a deeper difference of literary taste or judgment. Tolkien or Dyson won't budge. The dialogue is joyfully elevated. Lewis presses in deeper, a twinkle in his eye. The game is on!

Handled well, our disagreements can be both enjoyable and productive. They can deepen our relationships rather than destroy them—and can deepen us along the way.

---

4 George Watson, "The Art of Disagreement: C.S. Lewis (1898-1963)," *The Hudson Review* 48.2 (1995), p. 239.

The problem is that today, both in the broader culture and in the church, we are *not* handling disagreement well.

Part of the reason is surely the climate of increased outrage we inhabit. Cancel culture is everywhere. On social media, for example, the vices that make for unhealthy disagreement are not only tolerated but *rewarded*. Whether we realize it or not, the algorithms are playing off of envy, anger, and narcissism. Even those who steer clear of social media live in a world that is increasingly shaped by it.

But the problem goes deeper than the current climate. Disagreement is by its nature *always* challenging because doing it well requires a combination of different virtues.

Hedgehogs and Rhinos

In social psychology, there is a theory about two contrasting ways in which people deal with disagreement. Essentially, about half of human beings act like rhinoceroses: the other half, like hedgehogs. Rhinos are aggressive, charging when threatened. Hedgehogs are more defensive, using their prickles as a shield. One book puts it like this:

"Just as animals respond differently to attack, so people react differently when hurt and angry. There are two major patterns of behaviour, and ... it would appear that the population is split roughly fifty-fifty. Half of the population are like the rhino: when they are angry, they let you know it. The other half of

the population are like the hedgehog: when they feel angry, they hide their feelings." [5]

Whether you adopt this exact framework or not, it draws attention to an important fact: when it comes to challenging conversations or relationships, we all have different temptations. So disagreement will challenge all of us in different ways.

If you are a rhino, healthy disagreement will be difficult because it requires more restraint than you would naturally be inclined to show. You may have moments when you *feel* like "charging," and it might even feel like the *right* thing to do—but you actually need to tap the brakes. (Often we realize this only afterwards, once the temperature has cooled!)

But if you're a hedgehog, healthy disagreement will be difficult because it requires more boldness than you would naturally be inclined to show. You may have moments when you *feel* like hiding, but you actually need to embrace the vulnerability of leaning forward into the disagreement. Where you would normally pull back, you have to *speak up*. This can be scary! It rubs against our natural preference for harmonious relationships.

To make matters worse, hedgehogs and rhinos will often be tempted to look down on each other while ignoring their own weakness. The opposing flaws will be obvious to us, while our own will seem small or invisible. A rhino might look at a hedgehog and say, "Why doesn't

---

5 Nicky and Sila Lee, *The Marriage Book: How to Build a Lasting Relationship* (Alpha International, 2000), p. 158.

he speak up more? I know he agrees, but he lacks the courage to say so!" Conversely, a hedgehog might look at a rhino and say, "Why is she so argumentative? She turns *everything* into a fight!" Both might be (partly) right. This is one way that outrage about disagreement can contribute to *further* disagreement and outrage, without us realizing it.

The truth is that we *all* have some work to do. Healthy disagreement will draw all of us beyond our natural strengths. It will require stretching into new (often uncomfortable) territory.

For this reason, the ability to engage in healthy disagreement is a good general test of maturity. If you want to see how much self-awareness someone has, just watch how they respond to a good old-fashioned disagreement.

But Why Is Disagreement So *Annoying*?

Many of us love the idea of healthy disagreement in principle. The trouble is that in the heat of the moment we tend to get agitated and either go into rhino-like attack mode or hedgehog-like retreat mode. Why is disagreement so difficult, so *annoying*? Why does it create such an unpleasant feeling of cognitive dissonance?

Jonathan Haidt has written a fantastic book that helps us understand our disagreements. One of his insights is that we are, by nature, wired to be intensely loyal to a tribe: "People are *groupish*. We love to join teams, clubs, leagues, and fraternities."[6] Furthermore, he points out that most of our disagreements actually stem from gut intuition, not rational reflection.

The result of this is that human psychology is not well suited to conduct disagreement in a calm, rational, dispassionate way. Rather, we are profoundly shaped by social and emotional factors. We will often *feel* disagreements as a kind of threat to our broader identity. They trigger reactions deep down inside us, many of which we may not even be aware of.

For example, have you ever been in disagreement and found yourself having a thought like this: "Why in the world do they think *that*? What is *wrong* with them?!"

There is a reason why that feeling arises. It's part of your psychology. That feeling exists for a purpose. It's not all bad.

But we have to be reflective about what is going on inside us during our disagreements. This can help us to approach disagreements more carefully and more proactively.

And learning to have healthier disagreement is crucial because the stakes are very high.

Unhealthy Disagreement Discredits the Gospel
Western culture is increasingly polarized and polarizing, and if this trend doesn't stop or at least slow down, the consequences may be severe. Some

---

6 Jonathan Haidt, *The Righteous Mind: Why Good People Are Divided by Politics and Religion* (Vintage, 2012), p. 221.

even warn that in the United States our disagreements are growing so extreme that secession is a viable possibility.[7] More personally, most of us can recognize the role that unhealthy disagreement has played in our relationships—sometimes with the people who are closest to us.

The need to learn the art of disagreeing well is an especially poignant challenge for those of us who are followers of Christ, because failure in this area often discredits our witness to the gospel. In John 13, Jesus taught that it is our *love* (not our gifts or resources) that will ultimately gain the notice of the world: "By this all people will know that you are my disciples, if you have love for one another" (John 13:35). Four chapters later, in his famous high-priestly prayer, he prayed for our unity with a view to how this impacts the surrounding world: "… that they may all be one, just as you, Father, are in me, and I in you, that they also may be in us, so that the world may believe that you have sent me" (17:21).

The simple lesson is this: how we Christians treat each other matters. The world is watching. When we conduct disagreements without love and without appreciation of our broader unity, we become a hindrance to the gospel. We put a stumbling block before the watching world. That is the challenge. Yet, at the very same time, our disagreements present us with an opportunity. If we can learn how to love each other amid our differences, our very disagreements can commend the reality of Christ to those around us.

---

7 David French, *Divided We Fall: America's Secession Threat and How to Restore Our Nation* (St. Martins, 2020).

The stakes really are that high. How we disagree affects eternal souls. No wonder that Paul addressed a disagreement among early Christians that had led to a strained relationship by urging the two people involved to "agree in the Lord" (Philippians 4:2). To how many Christians today would Paul have to give the same appeal?

I remember hearing about a football team in which the wide receivers and the running backs were having a disagreement. The wide receivers thought the team were running the ball too much. The running backs thought they were passing too much. The disagreement turned into rivalry, then pranks, and then sabotaging one another. Trust fell apart, and the team lost games as a result.

This is a tragic illustration of what too often happens in the church. When our disagreements go sour, it impedes our larger mission. The gospel itself is affected. I especially grieve at the testimonies I hear from younger people of how lovelessness in the church has complicated their perception of Christianity.

Imagine a better scenario. Picture a large family gathered around the table at Thanksgiving. The meal is over. Chairs are pushed back, and conversation naturally turns to a topic of deep-seated disagreement. Yet the discussion proceeds without painful anxiety or personal acrimony. Points are argued vigorously but without shouting or disdain. There is a feeling of freedom—even at times a kind of joy. When all is said and done, the disagreements remain—but so do the friendships.

Wouldn't it be wonderful to be a part of more conversations like this? Wouldn't our world be a better place if we could do this better? How do we get there?

The Plan and a Model

In the first two chapters of this book, we consider kindness and courage. These two virtues lay a foundation for healthy disagreement. Both are needed: kindness without courage is too flimsy; courage without kindness is too brash. Only by *combining* courage and kindness can we arrive at healthy disagreement.

Then we get more practical. Chapter 3 covers listening: the more receptive part of disagreement. Chapter 4 covers persuasion: the more proactive part of disagreement. My hope is that these chapters provide you with an array of strategies for how difficult conversations can actually move forward—for how to make real progress when you feel stuck in a disagreement.

Obviously there is much else to say. But my hope is that this little book will help healthy disagreement feel a little less intimidating for you—a little more intelligible, more manageable. I hope you finish it feeling "I can do this! This can work."

Two suggestions as you read: first, think right now of a disagreement that you are currently navigating in your life. As you work through the following chapters, keep bearing it in mind and see what you can learn to approach that situation better. Second, remember to focus more on what *you* can learn and not what *others* need to learn. (Disregarding this is a temptation for all of us!)

Here's a final image before we dive in. One of my favorite stories in Scripture is the martyrdom of Stephen in Acts 7. I don't know why, but the courage of martyrs often makes me emotional. I can hardly talk about them without getting choked up. More on that in chapter 2.

Stephen provides us with a model of courage. He stands his ground against an angry mob. He is blunt in his speech: "You stiff-necked people, uncircumcised in heart and ears, you always resist the Holy Spirit" (Acts 7:51). Now, let's be clear: these bracing words are not a model for everyday, run-of-the-mill conversations! Stephen was facing an exceptionally hostile crowd, and the very gospel was at stake. Yet Stephen's unwillingness to back down is inspiring. To disagree well, we must be willing to stand our ground as well—even if it costs us our lives.

At the same time, Stephen is not retaliatory or vindictive. He does not return stone for stone. Note his final words: "Lord, do not hold this sin against them" (7:60). These words provide a window into Stephen's heart. *Even while being murdered*, he has no malice. He stands his ground against those attacking him, but he also prays for them. Though it's an extreme example, this gives us a model for how to approach disagreements in our lives. We, too, are called to love and pray for our fiercest enemies.

How does Stephen do this? I believe the answer is that he keeps his eyes on Jesus: "He, full of the Holy Spirit, gazed into heaven and saw the glory of God, and Jesus standing at the right hand of God" (v 55).

Just imagine it! Stephen is surrounded by a raging, vicious mob. Stones are being hurled at him. But Stephen is not looking at the stones. He lifts his gaze beyond his circumstances to see Christ in his heavenly glory.

Friends, this is our great need as well. We cannot manufacture within ourselves the blend of virtues needed for healthy disagreement. But when we look to Jesus, his kindness and courage flow into us, enabling us to speak the truth courageously but to do so with love in our hearts.

Whatever kinds of disagreements you are facing, I pray this book would ultimately direct you to Christ. There is nothing so beautiful as the character of Jesus. He is the most courageous person who ever lived, as well as the most compassionate. To encounter him is enthralling. He pours his love and grace into our hearts, empowering us to face seemingly impossible situations.

Jesus, teach us how to disagree with your courage and your compassion flowing through our hearts!

Discussion Questions

1. Is disagreement getting worse in modern society? If so, what do you think is causing that?

2. Have you ever witnessed disagreement to be destructive in your life or the life of someone you know? What was the result?

3. In your own experience, what has made the difference between productive disagreements and unhealthy disagreements?

CHAPTER ONE

KINDNESS

The hero of Fyodor Dostoevsky's novel *The Brothers Karamazov* is a 20-year-old young man named Alyosha. He is an unusual hero. He doesn't do much. In contrast to the bolder characters around him, he is often quiet and receptive, observing their arguments and actions without response.

Yet when all the dust settles, it is what is represented by Alyosha that triumphs in the novel. His sincerity, simple faith, and love for others continually redeems those around him. Above all, what stands out is Alyosha's *lack of contempt* for the other characters, even in their wretchedness. He does not despise others. He does not consider himself above them. He exemplifies the counsel he receives from a wise character, which sheds light on the redemptive power of love:

> *"At some thoughts one stands perplexed, especially at the sight of men's sin, and wonders whether one should use force or humble love. Always decide to use humble love. If you resolve on that once and for all,*

you may subdue the whole world. Loving humility is marvelously strong, the strongest of all things. There is nothing else like it."[8]

When we are faced with terrible evil, we are often perplexed. We wonder if we need to abandon humility and kindness and instead rely on force. Indeed, we often face this temptation even in smaller disagreements. Dostoevsky is saying no, love is always the strongest way to oppose evil and promote truth. Alyosha's simple kindness illustrates this profound reality.

It is hard to deny the beauty of the redemptive power of kindness. Even in our surrounding culture, while outrage and snark are escalating around us, there is also a thirst for sincere kindness. Consider the popularity of TV personalities such as Mr. Rogers and Ted Lasso. When we see real kindness, we sense its goodness.

However, kindness is complicated. It is not formulaic. It's often difficult to know how kindness relates to other virtues and what it even looks like in the complexities of real life in the modern world. In the church, there is much disagreement about kindness. In some circles, appeals to kindness are seen as weakness; in others, there are deep-seated differences as to what kindness should look like. In this chapter, let's clarify what role kindness can play in our disagreements.

8 Fyodor Dostoyevsky, *The Brothers Karamazov*, trans. Constance Garnett (Signet Classic, 1958), p. 309.

The Value of Kindness

Several years ago I started a ministry on YouTube. Over the years I have had the privilege of being in dialogue with all kinds of different people, and I have learned a lot along the way about how disagreement can go well or go poorly. Sadly, it's very easy for it to go poorly! And I have certainly made a lot of my own mistakes along the way.

Perhaps my deepest conviction resulting from these experiences is that kindness in dialogue is powerful. In my time on YouTube, I have imperfectly but sincerely sought to exhibit kindness to others. I've also gotten to know many sincerely kind people from other viewpoints. What I have discovered is that kindness opens up not only relational doors but intellectual doors. In other words, it helps us not only to like each other more but to understand each other better.

When we sincerely wish others well, it comes across. People can tell. Similarly, when what is in your heart toward someone is contempt and a "rolling of the eyes" attitude, this also will come across. People usually pick up on what is going on in our hearts as we talk to them. They can feel either our respect or our disdain.

When someone senses that we have goodwill and respect for them, it enables them to lower their defenses and really hear what we are saying. Sincere kindness can therefore help us make progress in a disagreement. It helps unmake caricatures and promote understanding of what the other side is saying. Someone once said, in the context of preaching, that "unless love is felt, the message is not heard." So it is in our conversations.

The next time you are approaching a conversation you anticipate being difficult, take time to pray for the person with whom you disagree. Get your heart into a place where you genuinely wish them well. Pray earnest blessings on them. Humble yourself before them. Try to lean toward them with genuine openness, showing respect for their dignity and complexity as a person made in the image of God.

This is difficult to do because during a disagreement, we will generally be tempted to place the other party into a category based on the nature of our disagreement—to see them as on the "other side." We must work actively to remember their humanity and avoid "othering" them. We must seek the sincerity of Alyosha—to avoid despising them no matter what flaws they may have or what our concerns may be.

Two things can help you preserve a heart of respect and kindness toward those with whom you differ. First, avoid speaking contemptuously about them to others. It is difficult to switch gears in your heart orientation to someone when you transition from speaking about them to speaking to them. If you speak respectfully about them to others, it is more natural to do so in their presence.

Second, give consideration to the experiences (and above all the suffering) that may stand *behind* their disagreement with you. They have not randomly arrived upon their views. Particular events have shaped them. There is often more pain and fear going on in the people around us than we can realize. Bearing this in mind may not change the disagreement, but it can give us more compassion along the way.

Try this out: the next time you are in a difficult conversation, seek with all your heart to wish the other person well while you are talking. The results might amaze you.

What are other ways in which we might show kindness in our disagreements? First, offer prayer. In ministry I have often been overwhelmed by the amount of pain in peoples' lives. Sometimes the thought comes, "What can I possibly do to help?" In those moments, I have found that offering prayer is an amazingly effective resource. We don't need to be sufficient in ourselves. We just commend them to God and ask him to intervene. God can touch people in ways we cannot.

The person with whom you disagree may not be open to you praying for them, or it might feel condescending. But you can still pray for them privately. And I am regularly amazed at how often people *are* okay with us praying for them, including some who may not even believe in prayer. In my time when offering to pray for people, I actually don't recall a single time when someone has rejected the offer. This is a way to show kindness even when you disagree.

A second way we can show kindness even amid disagreement is through encouraging words. People need encouragement more than we are likely to notice. Sometimes, we simply forget to encourage people. At other times, we are with people who appear successful or confident, and we don't realize that they still need encouragement. So it helps to have an intentional plan. A simple step, like a planned daily or weekly text message of encouragement, can go a long way.

In fact, as I have practiced this in my own life, I have been amazed at how frequently someone writes back by saying something like "This came at exactly the right time" or "I really needed to hear that today." I've concluded that *most* people, *most* of the time, need encouragement. When you have a disagreement with someone, speak encouraging words and see how it might open up doorways.

The Rationale for Kindness

But *should* we do this at all? What about those people who are extremely difficult to talk to, or whose perspectives are so evil they need to be rebuked? There are times for avoidance and rebuke, and kindness is not contrary to those actions. More on that in a bit. But first, we need to see the biblical rationale for kindness.

As we have said, kindness is controversial. A few years ago, for example, the word "winsomeness" triggered various debates. Granted, winsomeness and kindness are not identical terms, but a lot of the concerns about winsomeness are also relevant here.

Some people seem concerned that too much focus on being winsome or kind can lead us to compromise or to avoid saying hard truths. That can certainly happen, and I believe we can and should learn from critiques like these. However, these potential dangers do not mean that all focus on kindness is misplaced. Ultimately, we must recognize that for Christians, kindness is not merely a strategy but a matter of obedience to the New Testament.

Kindness is one of the fruits of the Spirit (Galatians 5:22). In Ephesians 4:32, we are called to "be kind to one another, tenderhearted, forgiving one another, as God in Christ forgave you." Would that Christians today were known for our tender-heartedness! (Again, this must be conjoined with other virtues as well, as we will consider in the next chapter.)

Someone might object that Ephesians 4:32 is addressing our demeanor toward other Christians, not toward the hostile world around us. But consider the kind of speech and attitude toward non-Christians that is mandated in passages like these:

> Show perfect courtesy toward all people. (Titus 3:2)

> Let your speech always be gracious, seasoned with salt.
> (Colossians 4:6)

> Make a defense ... with gentleness and respect.
> (1 Peter 3:15)

These commandments were not given in the context of peaceful, easy relationships. Christians in the 1st century faced a hostile surrounding culture. Indeed, the call to gentleness and respect in 1 Peter 3:15 mentions a context of slander and reviling: "... so that, when you are slandered, those who revile your good behavior in Christ may be put to shame" (v 16).

So we are not called to practice kindness just to one another or just to win over others; we are called to practice kindness toward those who are not won over and who are actively persecuting us.

For this reason, kindness is not weakness. It will take all the strength you have! Again, think of Stephen praying for those stoning him. We can only do this in the power of the Holy Spirit.

This is the Alyosha-like redemptive power of love. This is the way of Christ: "When he was reviled, he did not revile in return; when he suffered, he did not threaten, but continued entrusting himself to him who judges justly" (2:23). The pinnacle expression of this came at the cross, where Christ conquered evil through humility, obedience, and non-retaliation.

When we are tempted to leave off kindness because we feel threatened by evil, it helps to remember the character Boromir in *The Lord of the Rings*. Boromir has a good goal: he wants to destroy the evil represented by the ring of power. But Boromir wants to use the ring to accomplish this. Because of this, he unwittingly becomes involved in evil himself. The end does not justify the means.

We can never use evil to fight against evil. The only way is to maintain integrity, which includes kindness. In the end, from the perspective of heaven, it is always the Alyoshas of the world who end up the heroes.

Ultimately, this is the message of the gospel itself. God has shown kindness to us: "When the goodness and loving kindness of God our Savior appeared, he saved us, not because of works done by us in righteousness, but according to his own mercy" (Titus 3:4-5). To be a Christian is to receive the *kindness* of God: the salvation he has provided, out of sheer mercy, through Christ. If God's strategy for bringing goodness into our world is through love, mercy, and kindness, how can we turn aside to any other way?

A Clarification about Kindness

But at this point, a clarification is absolutely necessary: kindness does not mean the absence of discernment. Kindness is not being a doormat. Kindness is consistent with toughness and shrewdness.

Therefore, when the disagreement you are facing is with an evil person who is seeking to harm you, it is right to protect yourself. You matter to God. You should take all reasonable steps to take care of yourself (as well as those in your care), and this is not at odds with kindness. Kindness is not at odds with getting a restraining order or blocking someone on social media or withdrawing from a relationship. Sometimes these are necessary steps, for all parties concerned. Wishing people well does not mean we must always maintain a relationship.

The necessity of non-engagement and withdrawal comes up often in Paul's letters to Timothy and Titus. I think of this as *the spiritual discipline of ignoring people*. It sounds strange, but it is biblical: "As for a person who stirs up division, after warning him once and then twice, have nothing more to do with him, knowing that such a person is warped and sinful; he is self-condemned" (Titus 3:10-11). Jesus gives a similar commandment to those he sends out: "If anyone will not receive you or listen to your words, shake off the dust from your feet when you leave that house or town" (Matthew 10:14).

This is a lesson that many of us are slow to learn, but it is so important. There are evil people in this world. We should be kind but not naïve. There is a time to turn away. Again, consider the wisdom of Jesus' words: "I am sending you out as sheep in the midst of wolves, so be wise as serpents and innocent as doves" (Matthew 10:16). If you are experiencing a difficult disagreement and you are not certain whether or not you should persist in it or withdraw, here are some questions that might be helpful to consider:

- Does this person's behavior suggest that engaging with them has a realistic chance of being productive?

- Is addressing a disagreement likely to create further harm?

- Do I have any formal obligations that require me to resolve this difference, or can it be left unresolved without negligence?

- Could a season of waiting or reflection be beneficial before working through a particular disagreement?

Often it helps to involve wise friends who can help you think through the best approach. This is not formulaic or easy. Remember that God is a loving Father, who cares for you.

When Kindness Is Met with Malice

What do we do when our kindness is met with malice? We know that we are called not to retaliate, and we know that we may need to disengage from that person—but now what? How do we endure the unkindness of the world without being tainted? How do we retain an Alyosha-like purity?

The only answer is Jesus. Jesus has a special place in his heart for those who are being maligned. The people discarded and despised by our world are *especially* precious to him. We can go to him, finding strength in his promises and his presence.

At times I have felt the psychological effects of the nastiness of social-media attacks. Even though I've grown calloused enough that it doesn't hurt me, in some way it still *weighs* on me. It feels dark and heavy. You probably have, or have had, disagreements like that in your life. Sometimes kindness can open a door for progress—but at other times, there is nothing you can do.

In those moments, it helps to remember the wonderful promise of Matthew 5:11-12:

> *Blessed are you when others revile you and persecute you and utter all kinds of evil against you falsely on my account. Rejoice and be glad, for your reward is great in heaven, for so they persecuted the prophets who were before you.*

There are two great comforts in this blessing. One is forward-looking, concerning our joy: "... for your reward is great in heaven." The second is backward-looking, concerning our identity: "... for so they persecuted the prophets who were before you." What happiness! When your kindness is met with reviling, you are now associated with the great tradition of righteous sufferers, stretching back to Abel at the beginning of the human story. And the happy results will last forever, stretching forward into eternity.

We have every reason to follow Christ in practicing kindness to those around us. When you are reviled, do not revile in return. Bless those who curse you. Keep an open heart, even in bitter disagreement. Be like Alyosha, despising no one, wishing well to all. This is what Christ can do in and for you.

Jesus, give us wisdom to know what kindness looks like and strength to show kindness to everyone, no matter what we are facing!

Discussion Questions

1. How do Christians disagree about kindness today? What passages in the New Testament can you think of that are relevant to these disagreements?

2. Have you ever observed kindness "open a door" toward a better understanding and dialogue between two opposing views? What happened?

3. In your own life, how do you know when to withdraw from a person who disagrees with you, and when to keep talking?

CHAPTER TWO

COURAGE

Perhaps my favorite aspect of the character of Christ is that he does not back down from the Pharisees. Even when the temperature is raised to the point at which they are seeking to crucify him, he does not yield, not even the tiniest bit. He continually speaks the truth to them, even though it enrages them. He does not mince words.

This is an essential counterpoint to the last chapter. Kindness *alone* is not enough. If you are in a difficult disagreement and your *only* goal is to show kindness, you will be imbalanced: overfocused on being conciliatory to the detriment of speaking the truth. We need to balance kindness (commitment to the person) with courage (commitment to the truth).

Remaining steadfast in disagreement (as Christ does with the Pharisees) *without giving way to unkindness* is difficult and rare. But when we see it, it is beautiful. True courage is thrilling. None of us want to be a pushover. That is not attractive or noble. We want to be the kind of people who stand firm in our convictions, come what may.

This is so important to remember in our own disagreements. At times we will be tempted to feel guilt when someone is upset with us. It is easy to assume that if our words are not well received, we must have done something wrong. And it is good to always be open to considering this. But there are times when we must simply hold our ground. When you are standing on the truth, don't let anyone push you around. When your conscience directs you to speak up, don't let anyone silence you!

In *The Lord of the Rings*, the character Éowyn is confronted by a terrifying evil power that threatens her with horrible torment:

> "*Come not between the Nazgûl and his prey! Or he will not slay thee in thy turn. He will bear thee away to the houses of lamentation, beyond all darkness, where thy flesh shall be devoured, and thy shrivelled mind be left naked to the Lidless Eye.*'
>
> "*A sword rang as it was drawn. [Éowyn answered] 'Do what you will; but I will hinder it, if I may.*'"[9]

I love Éowyn's response here: "Do what you will." It is noble and thrilling to stand firm against evil like this, without regard for consequences. We all sense the beauty of this kind of courage. We all want to be like this.

---

9 J.R.R. Tolkien, *The Lord of the Rings* (Houghton Mifflin, 2004),
    p. 841.

Let this thought land upon your heart: God has battles for *you* to fight. There are conversations and situations in which you, like Éoywn, will need to stand your ground and not yield one tiny inch. There are evils that will stand against you, against which you must say, "Do what you will; but I will hinder it, if I may." How do you find this kind of courage?

In this chapter we will learn two lessons about courage: first, courage is vulnerable; second, courage is beautiful. This will help us consider the role that courage plays in our disagreements and pursue more of it in our lives.

Courage Is Vulnerable

There is a lot of fake courage in the world. One example is when people boldly denounce their ideological enemies on social media but do it largely for the approval of their own fanbase. Another is when preachers rail loudly against the sins of the culture but avoid sins within the church. This is a faux courage because, while it might feel grand or defiant, there is actually very little cost. Typically it earns applause.

Real courage doesn't feel macho. It feels vulnerable. True courage will often lead you to decisions and actions that *don't* merit any applause; and it will often take more courage to disagree with your friends than with your enemies.

For example, imagine you are out to lunch with several coworkers. A current event arises as a topic of conversation. A passionate opinion is stated by several others on the assumption that everyone else already agrees. But in your heart of hearts, you *don't* agree, and you feel the issue is deeply important. What should you do? When and how do you disrupt the assumption of agreement in the most helpful way?

Depending on your personality and the nature of the issue, you might be tempted to remain silent. And, of course, there are many times in which remaining silent may be prudent.

Not every issue is a hill to die on. Life and relationships require constantly "triaging" issues and living peaceably amid our differences on smaller matters.[10]

But sometimes it *is* worth speaking up. And when these moments come, we will need courage. Engaging in an active disagreement is often uncomfortable and can come with a real cost. Again, it is wise to be cautious; silence is often the best course. But the temptation to *always* be silent is a real one, especially for those of us who are more hedgehog than rhino.

If you want to see just how vulnerable being courageous can be, consider Jesus himself—particularly when he is on route to the cross. Consider how all the disciples abandoned him. Consider how he silently endured mockery and contempt. Consider how misunderstood and despised he was. Courage is often lonely like this!

I love the scene in *The Hobbit* when the character Bilbo

---

10 For help in discerning how to rank different issues, see my book *Finding the Right Hills to Die On: The Case for Theological Triage* (Crossway, 2020).

is traveling down through a tunnel to face the dragon Smaug. As he gets close, he sees smoke rising up and he hears the deep rumbling noise of the dragon snoring. Tolkien writes:

"It was at this point that Bilbo stopped. Going on from there was the bravest thing he ever did. The tremendous things that happened afterward were as nothing compared to it. He fought the real battle in the tunnel alone, before he ever saw the vast danger that lay in wait."[11]

In every one of our hearts, that battle for courage will be fought and won in quiet moments like this, when no one is watching. Courage will be a decision made down in the deepest places of our soul. We may not even be *aware* we are exhibiting courage.

Part of the reason courage feels vulnerable is that it is often forged in the context of decisions the outcomes of which are uncertain to us. We genuinely don't know what will happen. We are not in control. It takes courage to embrace what we believe is right without any guarantee of success.

And, of course, it takes even more courage to do so when we expect that success *won't* be the outcome. In the novel *To Kill a Mockingbird*, the lawyer Atticus Finch has a discussion with his daughter about a woman who has made a costly decision:

"I wanted you to see what real courage is, instead of getting the idea that courage is a man with a gun in

---

11 J.R.R. Tolkien, *The Hobbit* (Houghton Mifflin, 1966), p. 198.

his hand. It's when you know you're licked before you
begin, but you begin anyway and see it through no
matter what." [12]

There are few actions more vulnerable in life than entering a fight you know you will probably lose. But true courage often puts us in a position like this, where we must disregard consequences and plow ahead in the direction we know to be right. Think of Queen Esther deciding to speak out on behalf of the Jewish people, despite not knowing whether or not it would cost her her own life: "If I perish, I perish" (Esther 4:16). All of us will face moments when we will find ourselves needing to say, in effect, "If I perish, I perish."

The Role of Courage in Disagreement

How does the vulnerability of courage play out in our disagreements? First, courage will often summon us to *overcome conflict avoidance*. As I've said, of course avoidance is wise—sometimes. But there are times when we avoid certain topics or people out of sheer cowardice. Ask yourself this question: are there people or issues you *talk to yourself about* and spend emotional energy *thinking about*, but you avoid *facing directly*? When you find yourself having lots of mental conversations with someone but avoiding them in real life, you probably need to do something!

But how do we know when a disagreement is important enough to engage with and when we should just keep silent (or at least be ready to back down once we have

---

12 Harper Lee, *To Kill a Mockingbird* (Grand Central, 1960), p. 149.

gently stated our position)? This is a complicated question, but these two questions are a good starting point:

1. Is the disagreement important to the cause of the gospel? For example, will the reputation of Christ suffer if the topic is not broached? When it comes to, say, preferences in worship songs, we are called to simply be flexible and "not to quarrel over opinions" (Romans 14:1). On the other hand, if a leader in the church is having an affair, avoiding confrontation damages the cause of the gospel. We must constantly be discerning how important any given issue is. (Again, I have written another book about that![13])

2. Is a disagreement likely to be productive? We have all known situations where engaging is only going to bring more strife. The truth is that life contains a lot of situations like this. We are often called to hold back, pray, and wait for an open door. Consider Proverbs 20:3: "It is an honor for a man to keep aloof from strife, but every fool will be quarreling." A wise person will constantly be considering not merely what is right but what is edifying and useful. This requires much restraint.

Courage can also manifest in our disagreements as *a willingness to apologize*. We tend to think that courage will be seen in rebuke and assertion, but often it takes more courage to admit a mistake. Apologizing takes courage because when we own up to something, it can

---

13 *Finding the Right Hills to Die On.*

be used against us. But no true progress can be made in our disagreements if we lack the humility and honesty to admit it when we are wrong.

A final way in which courage is needed in our disagreements is *when we face pressure to yield*. All of us will face temptations to give up on a conviction or opinion when in our genuine heart of hearts we don't believe we should.

Consider when you have made a difficult change (as a leader or in a relationship) and are facing a backlash for it. Psychologists discuss a stage involved in any true change called *maintenance*. This is after we have made a change, and others are reacting to it, and we are pressured to cave in. What is necessary at that point is to *maintain* the change, over and against the pressure. Often this stage is more difficult than the change itself.

I love the Tom Petty song, "I Won't Back Down." These simple lyrics convey an important quality of courage— to resolve that even faced with "the gates of hell," nevertheless "I won't back down."

This attitude will be needed in healthy disagreement. In that uncomfortable space of clashing perspectives, you will at times be tempted to yield to the opposing pressure. You will need courage to stand firm. It won't feel grandiose. It will feel quite vulnerable. It may not earn much applause.

In a healthy disagreement, courage means being willing to say difficult words. This does *not* mean saying whatever we feel like. Courage is not venting. On the contrary, true courage will require wisdom, restraint, and calculation. We must not wound others with reckless words. But courage will require us at times to speak words that are difficult.

John Mayer's song "Say" captures the vulnerability of what courage can feel like in a disagreement: that your hands may be shaking and your eyes may feel as though they are closing, but nevertheless you still, with "a heart wide open," "say what you need to say."

Picture a college student sitting down with a friend at lunch. There is something she needs to say, but she is afraid. The topic has never been broached in their relationship. It's new, uncomfortable territory. Her hands are trembling. Her heart is racing. She takes a deep breath, embraces the moment, and gently speaks up. This is courage!

Courage Is Freeing

But courage is not only vulnerable. There is also a kind of freedom and joy in it, and I want to finish this chapter by highlighting this aspect of courage because I think it deeply resonates with our hearts, and perhaps especially with the hearts of young men.

We all ache for a cause to live for. We are designed to spend our lives on something larger than our own comfort and pleasure. This is why so many young people, despite the prosperity and affluence that surround us in modern culture, are deeply restless. We long for something more—something transcendent that makes a demand of us.

For this reason, while courage is not easy, it is wonderful, because it lifts us away from self-concern. There is joy in the self-abandonment of courage—in finding a cause for which to lay down your life.

I love how Paul described his life in these terms. Note the words "if only" in Acts 20:24: "But I do not account my life of any value nor as precious to myself, *if only* I may finish my course and the ministry that I received from the Lord Jesus, to testify to the gospel of the grace of God." It's as though Paul is saying, *My life doesn't matter, if only X can happen*; or *I don't care about anything, as long as Y happens.*

What would you give your life for? Speaking personally, I want to give myself to the cause of renewal and revival in the church. I would die for that. Everything else is negotiable. I want to spend myself to help people find the assurance of the gospel in a time when there is so much destruction and despair.

What is it for you? About what do you say, "I consider my life worth nothing, if only I can do *that*?" Put another way, what would you gladly die for? Until we have identified this, we are not fully living. It's thrilling to give yourself with abandon to your life mission—that particular calling that God has placed on your life, which will advance his glory and his salvation in this world.

There is a scene in the book *That Hideous Strength* where the character Mark is taken captive and brought into a room in which there is a large Spanish crucifix on the ground. He is ordered to trample on it and insult it.

Mark is not a Christian. He thinks it's all nonsense. But somehow he knows this is wrong.

And in that instant, he overcomes the fears that have controlled him for his entire life. He reasons, "Why not go down with the ship?" and refuses to stamp on the crucifix. And it is at that moment that his soul is at last born.[14]

There is a sense in which, when your find your courage, your find your true self.

In the disagreements you are facing, where is God calling you to move forward with joyful courage? Maybe it will look like broaching that uncomfortable topic you've been avoiding. Maybe it will involve revisiting a prior conversation where you caved in, to clarify your view and move the conversation forward. Maybe it will require holding the line against a bully or a troubled person who wants to guilt you into submission.

Whatever it is, be open to feedback from trusted friends about where your judgment might be off and remember to exhibit kindness along the way. But ultimately, you may need to say, with Tom Petty, "I won't back down." Remember, Jesus did not cave in one inch to the Pharisees.

Jesus Sees You

In the introduction we mentioned Stephen's martyrdom. There is another little detail in this passage that is fitting to note in conclusion to this chapter.

---

14 C.S. Lewis, *That Hideous Strength* (The Bodley Head, 1945).

Several years ago I was preaching on this passage and I noticed that Stephen sees Christ standing: "Behold, I see the heavens opened, and the Son of Man *standing* at the right hand of God" (Acts 7:56).

This is noteworthy because virtually everywhere that we see references to Christ at the right hand of God, he is *seated*: an indication of his authority and kingly rule. So why is he standing here?

I cannot be certain, but I wonder if Jesus is standing in recognition and honor of Stephen in this moment. He is proud of his martyrs. He is alertly watching.

Does this make your heart swell with longing to please Christ, as it does mine?

Let this happy thought wash over you: when you stand up courageously for Christ, as Stephen did, *Christ sees you as well.*

Jesus, give us courage, knowing you are watching from heaven!

Discussion Questions

1. In your own words, why is courage important amid disagreement? What happens in a disagreement when courage is lacking?

2. How do we know the difference between true courage and fake courage?

3. In your own life, how have you experienced being courageous to feel vulnerable? How have you experienced it as freeing?

CHAPTER THREE

LISTENING

Now that we have an overall framework for how to approach disagreements virtuously, let's get a bit more practical in how we can actually make progress in our disagreements. In this chapter we explore one particularly important and underrated skill: listening.

Listening is not high in our culture's list of values. For many, it may not be a value at all! But in the book of Proverbs, listening is one of the indelible marks of wisdom:

The way of a fool is right in his own eyes, but a wise man listens to advice. (Proverbs 12:15)

Whoever ignores instruction despises himself, but he who listens to reproof gains intelligence. (15:32)

A wise son hears his father's instruction, but a scoffer does not listen to rebuke. (13:1)

One reason that listening is so important is that most disagreements stem not from explicit differences of judgment but from deeper, unseen differences of value and presupposition. To really understand the other person (or people!) in a disagreement, we have to look *underneath* the explicit clash to see what hidden differences of worldview or past experience are at play.

In other words, in any disagreement, the other person is usually motivated by factors we cannot fully see. There are underlying, hidden fault lines of divergence that will only emerge with time. To make progress on the more obvious points of disagreement, we have to slow down to consider background differences of experience, values, and assumptions.

This is powerfully illustrated in this image of a man holding onto a woman at the edge of a cliff. The man cannot see the snake that is biting the woman's arm.

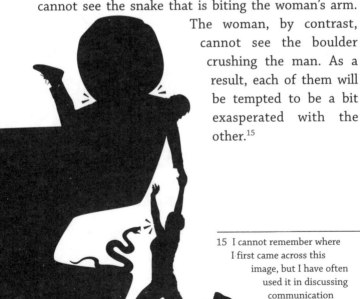

The woman, by contrast, cannot see the boulder crushing the man. As a result, each of them will be tempted to be a bit exasperated with the other.[15]

15 I cannot remember where I first came across this image, but I have often used it in discussing communication challenges.

The man might think, "Why can't she help pull herself up? Doesn't she care that I am being crushed?"

The woman might think, "Why won't he pull me up? Doesn't he care that I am getting bitten and about to fall?"

I suspect that something like this is happening in many of our disagreements. The only way to tell, and then to make progress, is through *listening*. And since a posture of sincere openheartedness toward others is at the core of healthy listening, we need to consider how to retain this heart posture amid the conflict of disagreement.

The Fine Art of Listening

Listening is surely one of the most undervalued skills in the world. Much conflict and suffering in the world stems from poor listening. Who knows what marriages might have been saved with better listening skills? Who knows what wars might have been avoided and what churches might not have split?

But listening is also a deep and complicated skill— one that we can keep growing in for our entire life. Listening does not mean agreeing, and it does not call for a blanket passivity in our conversations. In fact, communicating with different people calls for different styles of listening, since different people have different communication styles. When you are speaking with someone who runs on and on, active listening might require you to interrupt sometimes. When you are speaking with someone who is quieter, listening might require you to draw the person out with questions and to embrace periods of silence. Learning about our personalities and communication differences can be hugely helpful in any conversation, but perhaps particularly when it comes to navigating disagreement.

Listening takes energy. It's an active, responsive discipline. Someone once said that we are not really listening unless we are willing to be changed by what we hear. Good listening requires a posture of openness: a willingness to be maneuvered by the information we are receiving. Consider the words "open to reason" in James' description of heavenly wisdom: "the wisdom from above is first pure, then peaceable, gentle, *open to reason*, full of mercy and good fruits, impartial and sincere" (James 3:17). According to James, part of wisdom is the ability to be reasoned with. The Greek word here can be translated "reasonable, gentle, yielding" or even (in the King James Version) "able to be entreated." James is saying that a spiritually wise person is a person you can reach with an appeal or argument. They will listen to what you have to say.

A wise person will say things like...

- "Oh, I see! Okay."

- "Never mind! I was wrong!"

- "Ah, in *that* case, you're right."

- "Oh, *now* I understand."

- "I didn't realize that! Well, that changes things."

We have probably all witnessed a disagreement in which this does not happen. (Sadly, in my experience, this is more common than the alternative.) I imagine that you have experienced another person not really listening to what you are saying. Their mind is already made up. Your words bounce off their eardrums, but their meaning is lost. Whatever you say will not really make a dent in their preconceived interpretation. This is a distinctly unpleasant experience.

Failures to listen are a hugely aggravating factor in conflict and disagreement. Many times what really upsets someone is not a sheer difference of opinion but rather not feeling heard. In my role doing conflict mediation as a pastor, I've witnessed how frequently what a person wants is simply to be seen and respected. They don't need an answer so much as a hearing. This is true in many of our disagreements.

So when we feel stuck in a disagreement, sometimes a way forward can be found in practicing a deeper kind of listening. Consider Atticus Finch's advice to his daughter in *To Kill a Mockingbird*:

> *"If you can learn a simple trick, Scout, you'll get along a lot better with all kinds of folks. You never really understand a person until you consider things from his point of view ... until you climb into his skin and walk around in it."* [16]

This is a great way to conceive of skillful listening; we put ourselves in the other person's point of view, as much as we can. We consider how they are looking at the issue. How does their position make sense to *them*?

---

16 *To Kill a Mockingbird*, p. 39.

In my own situations of disagreement, I think one of the most helpful questions to ask is this: *how does their position relate to their worldview so as to form a coherent whole?* To the extent that we can learn to inhabit their concerns and values, we will more sympathetically understand their position.

One way to make progress in this way of listening is to cultivate a sincere curiosity about other perspectives. People genuinely think differently. Intelligent people come to radically different conclusions. When you think about it, this is fascinating. Rather than being threatened by these kinds of differences, we can learn to be curious about them.

Treat your disagreements like a science experiment. Give careful study to questions like these:

- What experiences have shaped this person?

- What background convictions undergird their position on the matter at hand?

- What fear or pain or hope might be influencing them in our disagreement?

- What social context are they in, and how does that shape their convictions?

In this way, curiosity is an important ingredient in healthy disagreement. This does not, of course, remove the disagreement. It simply helps us understand it better so that we are better positioned to make progress.

Strategies for Listening

It's worth considering some specific practices that can make us better listeners. First, be content to take your time in arriving at a final judgment about the disagreement. James 1:19 commands us to be "quick to hear, slow to speak, slow to anger." We are often just the opposite: slow to listen and quick to speak (and, for that matter, quick to anger!).

Healthy disagreement involves patience. Complicated differences simply take time to work through. It is a virtue to be able to say, "I have not made my mind up yet. I need to give it more consideration." Speedy judgments, by contrast, exacerbate disagreement.

For example, imagine you have just had a conversation with someone who thinks completely differently than you do. You were taken aback by the alien-like feel of the conversation. You were on completely different wavelengths. It was jarring. There will be a natural human tendency to make a judgment about the other person rather than living in the tension of uncertainty. We don't like not understanding someone. We would rather have easy boxes to put people in. It's more comfortable. But if we can learn to be curious about these kinds of deep-seated differences, rather than threatened by them, our disagreements will go much better.

Second, if you are more talkative by temperament, be careful not to overcrowd the conversation with your words. Some of those who are less assertive will need pauses in which to articulate their thoughts. Don't be threatened by not controlling the conversation. Be comfortable with silences. Embrace the back-and-forth rhythm of healthy communication. Learn to draw out the other speaker with unthreatened, unhurried space in which to think and communicate.

This kind of interplay in healthy listening and conversation will take shape differently when there are different personalities at play. For example, if you are less talkative by nature, you may need to speak up *more* in order to draw out the other speaker. We can leave lots of wiggle room for how this might play out differently, but this much is certain: if you are simply waiting to talk again when someone else is speaking, rather than actually valuing their contribution to the discussion, you are not doing it right!

We can learn how to communicate better by understanding different aspects of human personality and temperament. There are lots of different tools for learning about this, and none of them are beyond criticism. But the value in them lies in a simple fact: we are all different, and yet we tend to assume that *our* way of functioning is the *right* way. We can become better listeners by growing to appreciate how others experience, process, and communicate.

Third, ask clarifying questions. Asking questions of someone you disagree with is not compromise. It is a way to distill and clarify their ideas so that you can better understand them and thus clarify the nature of the disagreement. Consider questions that begin with phrases such as "Help me understand" or "I'm curious why..." or "What did you mean by...?" Another strategy is to summarize a position and then inquire if your summary is satisfactory: "What I think you are saying is... Have I got that right so far?"

Oftentimes questions are far more powerful than statements in advancing the truth in a conversation. This can even function (sometimes without you realizing it!) as a disarming way of challenging an opposing perspective.

Fourth, pay attention to little details, including the speaker's nonverbal communication. Good listening involves observing fine distinctions rather than clumping ideas together based on loose association. Good listeners treat each person on their own terms. They don't assume that two ideas or people are the *same* just because they are *similar*. Appreciating the complexity of reality means respecting the massive difference between *similar* and *identical*. Attentive listening honors the particularity of each person, and of each idea.

Imagine you are in a meeting at work. One of your coworkers makes a casual comment about his father being ill. He acts like it's not a big deal, but you recall he made a similar comment several weeks back. So just to err on the side of checking in, you approach him later to inquire more. His eyes well up with tears as he thanks you for asking. It turns out that it's a terminal illness and your coworker is completely overwhelmed and doesn't know what to do.

Without careful listening, this follow-up conversation would never have happened. Part of sensitivity to others is having our antennae out for little tiny comments that can give us opportunities like this. Someone might be communicating their need differently than we would. Their words may not be immediately obvious or alarming. But if we are listening, we will notice even little details.

Fifth, remember to give the benefit of the doubt. In any conversation, there will be some level of ambiguity in what the other party is saying. This presents us with a choice. We can fill in the blanks in a way that assumes the worst, or that assumes the best, or that lands somewhere in the middle. Make it your goal to assume the best, within reason. Err on the side of naïveté rather than cynicism. Not only is this much more productive, but it's actually a lot more fun. Your own heart will feel lighter and happier along the way. Wishing others well, and thinking well of them, is a happier way to live.

Finally, when you are confronted with strong or dogmatic opinions, remember that there may be pain lying underneath these views that you cannot see. A friend recently shared with me that trauma can have a role in producing dogmatism. As I reflected on this, it helped me understand the modern world so much better. The entire world is, in some respects, in trauma. Covid did a number on us. Perhaps this is one factor behind the increasing tendency toward fundamentalism, on all sides.

It will help you take disagreement less personally if you make allowance for this. We do not always see how others are suffering. What if the person you are disagreeing with is deeply depressed and you cannot tell? What if they are barely hanging on? Remembering this possibility will not remove the disagreement, but it can produce greater compassion and gentleness along the way. And the world deeply needs more gentleness right now.

Keeping an Open Heart during Conflict

But what about when our disagreement has boiled over into open conflict? It is difficult to listen well when trust and goodwill have been hindered. In extreme situations, where the disagreement is provoked by serious sin or wrongdoing, there will be a need for accountability and protecting yourself from further harm. In these situations, listening is not the primary need.

Nonetheless, it might be helpful to conclude this chapter by considering how we might respond well to conflict, keeping an open heart as much as possible toward the other party. Again, if the wrongdoing against you is severe, this may not apply. But in the more general kinds of conflict we often experience amid disagreement, here are five prayers that might enable us to keep the openhearted posture we have identified in this chapter as the essence of good listening.[17]

---

17 Some of the following material draws from my article "5 Prayers for When Conflict Strikes," www.thegospelcoalition.org/article/5-prayers-for-when-conflict-strikes/ (accessed May 29, 2024).

1. LORD, GIVE ME A HEART OF MERCY

Earlier we considered Ephesians 4:32:

Be kind to one another, tenderhearted, forgiving one another, as God in Christ forgave you.

Again, note this beautiful word "tenderhearted." We are called not merely to forgiveness and kindness but to a particular *quality* of forgiveness and kindness—one that is from the heart, tender, sincere, and warm.

When you are struggling to listen or keep an open heart to the other party in a conflict, it is good to pray for a heart of mercy. This does not mean you must lay aside legal redress or accountability for future wrongdoing. But it does mean that you desire reconciliation and fellowship more than "winning": that you seek to redirect evil and look for pathways by which to turn it to good—that you absorb pain in order to aim at restoration and peace. "A harvest of righteousness is sown in peace by those who make peace" (James 3:18).

To pray for a heart of mercy amid conflict can be excruciatingly difficult, especially if you've been sinned against. It feels a little bit like dying. It may require us to persevere in prayer for those who have wronged us and "pray until we've prayed," as the Puritans used to say. Above all, it will require a heart full of the Lord Jesus' own kindness, tenderheartedness, and forgiveness for us, from which we draw strength to practice the same.

2. LORD, HELP ME TO STAY POSITIVE AMID NEGATIVITY

It's easy to get sucked into negativity. The 19th-century philosopher Friedrich Nietzsche said, "Those who fight monsters should be careful lest they become monsters." Perhaps that is why Paul, after calling for Christians to pursue the restoration of a fellow believer who's fallen into a pattern of sin, immediately adds, "Keep watch on yourself, lest you too be tempted" (Galatians 6:1).

It's easy to react against a real problem but in the process become tainted by what we react against. For example, you rebuke someone who is being hotheaded or aggressive, and in doing so you find yourself getting a little heated. Or in sensing the pride of your neighbor, you find your own ego provoked. (Pride is essentially competitive.) Or when another party is constantly interrupting you, you give up on listening and start talking over them in return.

In order to keep unstained by the negativity and backbiting that conflict often engenders, we need to keep our eyes on Jesus. As the 19th-century pastor Robert Murray M'Cheyne put it:

"For every look at self—take ten looks at Christ! Live near to Jesus—and all things will appear little to you in comparison with eternal realities."[18]

When our disagreements are heated, we must keep our eyes on Jesus so that our discussions do not lead us into sin.

18 As quoted in Michael Reeves, *Rejoicing in Christ* (InterVarsity USA, 2015), p. 11.

3. LORD, HELP ME NOT TO TAKE THIS CRITICISM PERSONALLY
It's the most natural thing in the world to take criticism personally. It's as instinctive as flinching when a punch comes. But a defensive, self-referential spirit not only hinders our ability to serve; it is, in many respects, the opposite of serving. We cannot serve others, which is an essentially self-emptying act, when we are occupied with defending our own reputation or ego.

In fact, I have found that how we receive criticism is often one of the ripest opportunities for serving another person. When criticism comes, there is often something going on in the heart of the critic—something that many times has nothing to do with us. When our hearts are secure in Christ's love for us, we can better see these needs and respond to them—as well as humbly recognize when the criticism is fair.

4. LORD, GIVE ME HOPE FOR THIS PERSON'S RENEWAL
When we are in conflict with others, their flaws tend to loom large in our hearts and minds. It can become easy to assume evil in their motives ("He's deliberately trying to undermine me") or reduce them to a caricature of their sins ("She's just a gossip") or exaggerate their hurtful tendencies ("They *always* do that"). Being a good listener requires that we do not exaggerate others' vices and ignore their virtues. I find it helps to pray for God's vision for a person's progress in Christ and then ask for grace to genuinely hope in that vision.

Dostoevsky famously remarked that to love another person is to see them as God sees them. When we're in conflict with brothers or sisters in Christ, it can be helpful to envision them not as they currently are but as they will be after they've been worshiping around God's throne and among the angels for 100,000 years. Seeing people in this light not only informs our prayers for them; it also motivates and empowers those prayers.

5. LORD, SHOW ME MY OWN SIN

The default of our hearts toward self-justification can often lead us to neglect our own contribution to a conflict, or at least minimize it in proportion to the other person's contribution. In some conflicts one party may be the innocent lamb and the other the wicked wolf. But more often the blame can be sliced 90:10, or 80:20, or 50:50, or some other ratio in which both terms are greater than zero. And even in those rare situations of complete victimhood, it is healthy to remember that Jesus looked into Judas's eyes not with anger and retaliation but with sadness and love.

In order to not feel threatened by owning our own contribution to the conflict and to genuinely consider the other person's perspective, we need hearts that are full of the gospel. When we know that our sins have already been nailed to the cross—that our identity and standing does not hang in the balance to be determined by whether we "win" the conflict—it liberates us to examine our hearts and see how we might have contributed to the problems.

I recognize this is difficult! Again, if you are a victim of abuse, I am not talking to you. But in the midst of the ordinary conflicts of life that we all go through, we often have something to learn—*if we are able to keep listening.*

In your disagreements, keep an open heart for listening to what God is teaching you. Staying open and responsive is a pathway to wisdom, joy, and life.

Jesus, give us open hearts that are ready to hear what we need to hear from the conflicts of this life!

Discussion Questions

1. What does it feel like when someone is not listening carefully to you?

2. What skills have you found most helpful to better hear and understand different perspectives?

3. How do we know when we should learn something from a conflict vs. when we should disregard what the other party has said? Give an example from your own experiences or observations.

CHAPTER FOUR

PERSUASION

If listening is the more receptive aspect of conversation and dialogue, persuasion is the more proactive. Listening involves *understanding* someone; persuasion involves seeking to *move* them. In this chapter we will seek practical wisdom about this latter aspect of disagreement.

Persuasiveness simply means influencing others, particularly in their thoughts and opinions. It means being able to win someone over, reducing obstacles to agreement, and providing motivation for a change of mind. While some people are more naturally persuasive by temperament, all of us can learn strategies and techniques to grow in our ability to move and influence others.

In one scene of the movie *My Big Fat Greek Wedding*, Toula is discouraged by her father's stubbornness. She feels she will never change his mind. Her mother comforts her by saying, "The man may be the head of the household. But the woman is the neck, and she can turn the head whichever way she pleases."

This is a funny but effective way of describing the power of persuasion. If you are skilled at persuasion, you can find ways to make progress in seemingly intractable disagreements. Even when you feel outpowered and outgunned, you might find a way forward. If you've ever observed someone engage in effective persuasion, it's truly an art form to behold!

This is something we all should strive to learn about. It will make a huge difference in our disagreements.

Persuasion Is Good

Yet persuasion is a controversial topic in today's world. Some worry that it can easily slide into manipulation. Others are against imposing our ideas on others in a domineering way. These concerns are valid.

Many of us also have personal hesitations about persuasiveness because of our background or personality. Perhaps we don't want to appear argumentative, so we feel hesitant about really pressing a point. In the midst of a disagreement, we may feel an internal pressure to yield too quickly.

We can stack up many valid concerns about persuasion done badly. But we should not devalue persuasiveness itself. We can easily imagine scenarios where persuasion is absolutely critical: helping a friend who is considering suicide or attempting to encourage someone away from a hateful ideology. No one would say that persuasion is bad in those cases. The truth is that done rightly, persuasion is an act of love.

Therefore, so long as we remember the lessons from the last chapter about listening, we *should* seek to be as persuasive as we can be in any conflict. If we care about people, we should want to encourage them toward truth and wisdom. Even when no one changes their mind, attempts at persuasion help us understand one another better. Think of it like this: God has given you unique insights and experiences, and if you don't share them, you may be depriving others around you of what God wants to teach them through you.

Valuing persuasion is biblical. Proverbs portrays persuasive speech as part of wisdom: "The heart of the wise makes his speech judicious and adds persuasiveness to his lips" (Proverbs 16:23). The apostle Paul provides a good model of persuasive speech when he is on trial at the end of the book of Acts. His speeches to various civil authorities are filled with diplomacy, tact, firmness, and force:

> *Knowing that for many years you have been a judge over this nation, I cheerfully make my defense.*
> *(Acts 24:10, to Governor Felix)*

> *I consider myself fortunate that it is before you, King Agrippa, I am going to make my defense today against all the accusations of the Jews, especially because you are familiar with all the customs and controversies of the Jews. Therefore I beg you to listen to me patiently.*
> *(26:2-3, to King Agrippa)*

> But Paul said, "I am not out of my mind, most excellent
> Festus, but I am speaking true and rational words."
> > (v 25, when interrupted by Festus)

It's hard to dismiss someone who speaks cheerfully, respectfully, and reasonably, as Paul does here. This is a good way to think about what happens when you are persuasive; it makes it harder for people to dismiss you.

Persuasion Is Difficult

But persuasiveness is also difficult. It has never been harder to persuade people! I read an article recently in *The New Yorker* called, "Why Facts Don't Change Our Minds." It references studies conducted at Stanford University in the 1970s, documenting how hard it is for people to change their minds once they have formed an opinion. The point was to show that even when their beliefs are refuted by facts and evidence, people often refuse to revise them. The article commented:

> "Coming from a group of academics in the nineteen-seventies, the contention that people can't think straight was shocking. It isn't any longer. Thousands of subsequent experiments have confirmed (and elaborated on) this finding ... Any graduate student with a clipboard can demonstrate that reasonable-seeming people are often totally irrational."[19]

Most of us don't find this difficult to understand, especially as we observe the impact of social media and

19 www.newyorker.com/magazine/2017/02/27/why-facts-dont-change-our-minds (accessed May 29, 2024).

cable news throughout our society. If we are honest, perhaps we can even see this tendency in ourselves at times.

The truth is that mere facts and information often fail to move people. Yet when we are in a disagreement we often forget this, relying on sheer force of argument, oblivious to helpful ways to persuade people and the broader sociology of how people actually change their minds. The result is like a head-on collision: it's painful and unproductive.

Learning some simple principles of persuasion can dramatically help us influence those around us—even those who are seemingly stuck in their opinions. Let's consider eight strategies that might be useful.

1. BUILD TRUST

In ancient Greek rhetoric, the skill of persuasion was often broken down into three categories:

- *Logos* referred to the content of the speech; it's how the speaker uses *logic* to influence listeners.

- *Pathos* referred to the speaker's passion and appeal to feelings; it's how the speaker uses *emotion* to influence listeners.

- *Ethos* referred to the speaker's credibility; it's how the overall *trustworthiness* of the speaker influences listeners.

Obviously, all three are important. But which would you guess is *most* persuasive? Perhaps surprisingly, the answer is *ethos*.[20] We often assume that *what* we say is how we will move others. We think, in effect, "If my argument is sound, they will have to agree with it!" Or perhaps we assume that speaking well and with passion is what will win them. But the biggest ingredient in an act of persuasion is simpler: does the listener trust the speaker? And especially: does the listener feel that the speaker cares for their welfare?

Trust is absolutely essential in any act of communication. If the other person does not trust us, they will have their defenses up and very rarely can brilliant logic or powerful emotion break through such defenses. It's simply not how we are wired. Just think of yourself: when was the last time you were persuaded by the argument of a person you distrusted?

Obviously we cannot completely control whether others trust us. But we can do everything within our power not to give people reasons to distrust us. We can aim to speak sincerely, mindful of God, in the way that Paul describes his ministry: "as men of sincerity, as commissioned by God, in the sight of God we speak in Christ" (2 Corinthians 2:17). It's also sometimes possible to win back trust that has been lost. How can we do this?

a) Be willing to apologize and own mistakes or errors. Even simple admissions like "Oh, I see—I misunderstood" convey goodwill and honesty. If you never apologize,

---

20 Bryan Chapell, *Christ-Centered Preaching: Redeeming the Expository Sermon* (2nd ed.; Baker Academic, 2005), p. 34. Chapell outlines how this was Aristotle's view and how this has been confirmed in many modern studies.

you may be giving the other person reason to wonder whether you care about being right more than finding the truth. Even a slight suspicion of this damages trust.

b) Be appropriately candid about your aims in the disagreement. It's okay to have a goal in the conversation, but trust is diminished when the other party senses an agenda that is lurking under the surface rather than transparent. Sometimes it even helps to lay out your values or desires, saying something like "What I really hope to convince you of is..."

c) Be careful not to gossip about the person or triangulate them by bringing in a third party. Speak with them directly—ideally, face to face. A phone call or Zoom meeting might be a necessary back-up for some conversations, but written communication should generally be avoided because it is much less personal.

d) State your feelings. Be human. Be honest and free and relaxed, as much as you can. As appropriate, provide the other party with information about your background, your experiences, and your feelings about the topic. This requires vulnerability because you are making visible your subjectivity rather than relying on impersonal logic alone. Vulnerability breeds trust. It's astonishing how frequently you can win people over with a loving, sincere, transparent expression of the values that determine your thinking.

e) Have an open and loving heart toward the other person. There is simply no shortcut around this. People will be able to tell, sooner or later, whether your attitude toward them is sincere or sour. Ultimately, the only way to *appear* trustworthy is simply to *be* trustworthy. Therefore the most important way to persuade others is to have purity of heart and a transparent integrity.

2. USE TACTFUL SPEECH

In the heat of a disagreement, we are often instinctively defensive. We have our guard up against what the other party is saying. We feel as though their arguments and words are cannon balls being shot at us and that we have to raise our defensive walls to block them from landing.

It is extremely difficult to influence someone amid this dynamic. Again, logical arguments are virtually useless if the other party has their guard up. There will always be some way they can escape the force of an argument, if they desire to.

For this reason, we must begin by seeking to disarm the defensiveness of the other party. It's often wise to avoid leading off with adversarial language that immediately corrects or rebuts the other party (words like "but," "no," "however," and so on). Instead, try to "soften the blow" by leading off with gracious and conciliatory speech or by identifying a point of common ground before addressing remaining disagreement. Sentences that begin like the following can help your speech receive a better hearing:

- "A point of agreement is..."

- "One thing I appreciate about you is..."

- "I am glad we are talking about this because..."

- "This is an interesting conversation. One thing I am learning is…"

Don't follow these sentences with an adversarial word such as "but" or "however," which risks draining them of their power. Rather, simply move on to points of disagreement as additional, separate points.

There are two dangers here, however. One is making this general principle into an absolute rule. There are times when we need to say, like Paul, "By no means!" (Romans 3:4). In particular, when you are confronted with an assertion that is hateful, harsh, shocking, or evil, it may be necessary to respond with a more vigorous disagreement. Even there, though, seek to be wise and intentional with your speech, aiming to win that person over to the truth rather than just to denounce them.

The second danger is using tactful speech in a way that comes across as insincere. If it feels too canned, or if you are constantly smothering the other party with compliments, it can backfire and alienate them. So make it your goal to listen carefully to the other party, from the heart (as we discussed in the last chapter), so that conciliatory words are genuine and accurate.

3. HELP THEM SAVE FACE

There is an ancient figure of speech called *litotes*. Litotes is a form of understatement. Essentially, it means stating a positive by means of a negative. It was used to great effect by ancient orators and rhetoricians, like the Roman statesman Cicero (from whom we can learn much about persuasion). An example would be saying, "That Uber driver was not the best I ever had." Strictly speaking, this is an extremely mild statement. But no one wonders whether you are saying that this Uber driver was the second best or the third best. We understand that you are actually saying, though not in so many words, that this was a *bad* Uber driver.

In the context of a disagreement, using understatement like this can be a powerful way to make a point without making the other party feel unnecessarily confronted or embarrassed. Consider this example. You are disagreeing with your brother about how healthcare should be regulated, and he provides an absolutely horrendous argument to support his view. Instead of saying that his argument is horrendous, you say, "That was not the *best* argument I've heard you make for your position." This can be disarming because (a) it avoids *directly* calling his argument bad, and (b) it implies that your brother has made good arguments in the past. Sometimes this won't be strong enough, but at other times this can be an effective way to draw attention to the weakness of an argument.

Here's a more subtle example. Imagine you are having a conversation with your neighbor about who should replace the fence between your yards. With some forcefulness, he states, "You should pay for it; I don't even care if it gets replaced!"

You disagree. In fact, you have good reason to think he does care about the fence. Consider two possible ways to counter:

1. "I disagree with what you are saying; instead, we should split it 50/50. After all, I think you *do* care that it gets replaced."

2. "I hear what you are saying; what do you think about splitting it 50/50?"

The first statement is more strictly accurate regarding your thoughts about the situation. You *are*, in fact, disagreeing with him. And you *do* question his motives. But the second is more diplomatic. You are getting across the same information in a way that is less bracing to experience. No one likes having their motives questioned (this is generally a good thing to stay away from), and the words "I hear what you are saying" camouflage the fact that your proposal is adversarial to his.

I want to make clear that I am not advocating starting off all your sentences with the words "I hear what you are saying"! We have to be careful not to go too far or to fall short of telling the truth. Still, it is worth considering the most tactful possible way of making your point.

When we give thought to it, there are all kinds of ways like this to depressurize the situation for the other speaker. We should give consideration to how we can deflect attention off of them *personally*. It's been wisely observed that there is a difference between saying, "Your foot is too large for this shoe" and "Your shoe is too small for your foot." The former puts the focus and the implicit blame on the person; the latter takes the pressure off. When we are seeking to persuade someone, we should be mindful of how we can depressurize the situation so as to make it easy for them to agree with us.

The bottom line is that merely obliterating your opponent with powerful arguments is not the best way to persuade them. Rather, you have to help them "save face" in changing their mind. Don't merely burn down their house; point them to a safe exit door and make them feel good about walking through it.

4. BALANCE CRITICISM WITH PRAISE

The ability to balance criticism with points of appreciation and agreement is incredibly important in persuasion. It helps the other party not feel on the defensive by showing that your disagreement with them is measured, not wholesale. And it helps both parties keep the disagreement in its proper context.

Many of us have learned the power of this strategy when giving (or receiving) a job performance review; the person will learn more from critical points of feedback if we have also identified some positives. Just as the best rebuke comes only after many words of encouragement, so also the most persuasive expression of disagreement comes after identifying areas of common ground and agreement.

The 6th-century Christian Gregory the Great wrote a masterful book called *The Book of Pastoral Rule.* It is filled with wisdom about how to speak and lead with skillful persuasion. One particular example is his counsel about how pastors should correct the proud.

While Gregory's advice is geared toward how those in a leadership role (like pastors) seek to persuade, it is relevant to all kinds of disagreements. Essentially, Gregory points out that correction should be balanced with praise: "It is generally more useful to correct the proud if we combine a measure of praise with our correction."[21]

Gregory then develops this thought with two metaphors: just as unbroken horses must first be touched gently with the hand before they receive a whip, so the proud should be given a measure of praise at first so that they will receive correction they would otherwise scorn. Likewise, just as bitter medicine is mixed with a sweet flavor so that what can heal a deadly illness will not be spit out of the mouth, so our speech to the proud should be initially pleasing so that it is met with favor. Gregory is even willing to display a kind of deference to the proud, in the hope of winning them over:

> "It will generally be easier to persuade the proud that amendment is beneficial if we speak to them about their improvement as though it would help us rather than them ... We should convince them that their amendment is a favor to us."[22]

For all the sternness of Gregory's book, this advice is surprisingly accommodating! Essentially, he is stating that sometimes a correction can be stated as a personal request in order to make it "go down easier."

---

21 Gregory, *The Book of Pastoral Rule* 3.17, p. 133.
22 As above.

We shouldn't assume that we are always in the position Gregory is envisioning here (a pastor correcting a "proud" person!). But even in other contexts, the habit of avoiding direct criticism when possible can help us be more persuasive. Imagine, for example, that you are leading a small-group discussion. There is one particular person in the group (let's call him John) who is very talkative—so talkative, in fact, that no one gets a word in edgewise. He is not malicious; he is just oblivious to the effect of his speech on others. What do you do? Consider two possible ways to confront him:

1. "John, you are talking too much. No one else can get a word in. You need to talk less."

2. "John, I really need your help. It's really important to me to lead this group into an effective discussion. I would love to draw out some of the others in the group more. Do you think you can help me draw them out a bit? Sometimes we are going to have stay silent so they can have a turn."

The second appeal is going to be much easier for John to receive and therefore is much more likely to be persuasive.

I want to be careful here; it's possible to go too far with this. Again, our speech should be truthful and sincere. And there are times to be more blunt—especially if someone has not gotten the memo the first few times we have spoken with them. But generally speaking, it's good to offer corrections at first more subtly, indirectly, and with understatement, and only then crank it up if needed.

5. CALMLY IDENTIFY DISAGREEMENTS

When we are in the heat of a disagreement, it is easy to for emotion to cloud our ability to think logically. It is often helpful to pause, pull back from whatever we are feeling, and deliberately focus on facts and evidence. A calm, simple assertion of fact can bring clarity amid ambiguity, reduce the interpersonal pressure in a disagreement, and increase the other party's responsibility to interact with what you have said.

When doing this, it helps to be honest about the disagreements. Don't beat around the bush. Bring the disagreement out into the light, but do so calmly. It can sometimes feel threatening to identify a point of disagreement. Stating it in a factual, matter-of-fact way reinforces that it is safe to disagree and that the person's relationship with you is not at stake in your disagreement. Words like these can be powerful: "Am I right in gathering that where we disagree is...?"

This can be helpful because when we fail to identify where a particular disagreement lies, we often make assumptions about the other party's convictions. Many disagreements suffer from lack of clarity; the two sides don't actually *know* where they disagree, and thus they talk past one another. Calmly wading through a disagreement to identify where the real fault lines of difference lie often brings clarification.

In this process, it helps to seek to steelman the opposing position, rather than strawman it. In other words, put the best possible construction on it, such that the other person feels satisfied with how it has been represented, and only then embark on disagreement. You might say, for example, "We seem to agree on X and Y but have a disagreement about Z. On Z, your position seems to be... Mine, by contrast, is... Does this sound right to you?"

It's amazing how many disagreements are reduced by this kind of careful, clarifying work. Sometimes they can even evaporate altogether.

6. USE ARGUMENTS

It sounds so simple to say that we should use arguments to persuade people, but sometimes we forget. In the midst of a disagreement, we often find ourselves falling into making mere assertions. It's easier to emote than argue. Or we can rely on personal experience or an anecdote that will not be convincing for another person. It is good to learn the discipline of providing some facts, evidence, reasons, or arguments for our position. Even if the other party is not convinced by our arguments, merely advancing them places the onus on them to respond and show *why* they are not convinced.

It's especially hard to construct arguments for positions we think are obvious. I remember talking to a friend to help myself prepare for a debate. I casually referenced a particular point (that denying the filioque is not a first-rank heresy[23]). My friend challenged me: "That

---

23 It's not necessary to get into this here, but the filioque is part of the doctrine of the Trinity, the Christian conception of God. Essentially it states that the Holy Spirit proceeds from the Father and the Son. Historically, it has generally been affirmed by Western Christians and denied by Eastern Christians.

may be obvious to you, but it's not obvious to them"
[my opponents]. He was right. I was simply *assuming*
a point when it needed to be *argued for*. I had to circle
back and subject myself to the discipline of learning to
articulate *why* this belief seemed so obvious to me, in
case it came up in the debate. (Sure enough, it did.)

Sometimes we falsely assume that arguments are what
cause disagreements. But I think the opposite is closer
to the truth. Having an argument is not the same
as being argumentative; it is possible to state our
arguments tactfully and graciously. In fact, it's often
not having an argument that aggravates a disagreement.
When we take a position for granted because it seems
obvious to us, we can easily become frustrated that it's
not obvious to someone else. It takes discipline to slow
down and calmly think through what arguments might
persuade someone when it comes to the points that we
may not think *need* an argument. But doing that is far
more likely to advance the conversation than simply
asserting something and, in doing so, implying that all
right-thinking people would think the same.

The character Spock in *Star Trek* is known for especially
valuing and emphasizing logic. At one point in the
2009 Star Trek movie, Spock's father says, "Logic
offers a serenity humans seldom experience: the
control of feelings, so that they do not control you."
There is something profound about this; in the heat
of a disagreement, logic is *calming*. It gives serenity.
It helps you stay objective. Especially for those of
us who don't like conflict and are more emotionally
geared, deliberately focusing on the use of logic and

argumentation is one way not only to persuade the other party but to ensure that we are responding appropriately.

Of course, logic *alone* is not enough to persuade (see point 1!). But it is a resource to us in the process, especially when we feel the temperature of the conversation is escalating. The next time you are getting angry in a conversation, slow down, count to ten, and try to focus on *thinking*. This often clarifies how to move forward.

7. REITERATE YOUR GOALS

I once received some helpful advice about leadership amid conflict: most people are not *against* you; they are simply *for* themselves. This is usually true in disagreements; the other person probably cares more about them being right than you being wrong. Proving you wrong is just serving this larger goal. Thus, we tend to experience disagreements personally: when you disagree with someone, they think you are against them. You become a threat.

For this reason, it often helps in the course of a disagreement to reiterate your deepest goals and desires. You want the other party to understand that you are not their mortal enemy. You want to act in a way that makes clear that first and foremost, you are *for* the truth rather than *against them* personally.

I find that the simplest way to do this is simply to say it explicitly. Let's say you are in a disagreement with your friend about what forms of free speech should be allowed. The discussion is ramping up. At a critical moment, you preface your comments with a clarification:

"I am going to offer a different perspective, but I want to make clear I don't think you're my enemy here. I'm not against you. I think we're ultimately on the same team here. But I am trying to follow Christ to the best of my ability. That is the most important thing to me. That is why I want to share my concerns about..."

A reasonable person can experience this as disarming.

It can also be helpful, if appropriate to the relationship, to periodically affirm your personal respect and value for the other party as a person. This also helps your words receive a good hearing. You might say, for instance, "John, you definitely have my respect! I am trying to do a good job in this disagreement because of how much I value our friendship. One of the things on my heart is..." Again, a reasonable person will likely be able to hear your words with greater openness.

8. APPEAL TO SYMPATHIES ALREADY HELD

Nathan the prophet provides a brilliant example of how to effectively persuade someone in the context of confrontation. His (rather terrifying) task is to confront King David about his sin in committing adultery with Bathsheba and having her husband, Uriah, killed to cover it up. How does Nathan approach this? He does it indirectly, by telling a story about a poor man whose lamb was stolen by a more powerful man. On hearing the story, David is furious: "The man who has done this deserves to die" (2 Samuel 12:5). Only then does Nathan confront him: "You are the man!" (v 7).

I wonder how differently the conversation would have gone if Nathan had led off with confrontation? He was wise to arouse David's indignation and only *then* apply it to the king's own sin. Once his emotional response was triggered, David was less likely to minimize or deflect the guilt of his actions.

The prophet Amos does the same thing in confronting Israel. First, he announces God's judgment on the surrounding nations for their sins (Amos 1:1 – 2:3). God's people would have been cheering during these sections of the book. Only then, once their moral feelings have been engaged, are Judah and Israel given the exact same warning.

There is wisdom in this strategy. When you have to confront someone, don't lead off with "You are the man!" Instead, tell them a story. Appeal to convictions and emotions that they already have and then draw them into the situation you need to discuss.

Keeping an Open Mind as We Open Our Mouths

In this chapter we have sought to sketch out some strategies for persuasion. In all of this, though, we must remember our fallibility. When we are seeking to persuade others, we must be willing to consider that at times we might need to be persuaded to change ourselves! Especially when it comes to more complicated or peripheral matters, we must keep an open mind and consider what is being said to us, even as we seek to commend the truth as best we see it.

Nonetheless, persuasion is important in the current state of our world. Underneath the deep disagreements of modern culture, there is often pain and fear. Instead of feeling only threatened by the vitriolic nature of many public disagreements, we can see an opportunity. People are aching for truth and meaning. If they are not persuaded by good ideologies, they will be persuaded by bad ones.

We should, then, do everything in our power to win people to the truth. "Speaking the truth in love" (Ephesians 4:15) does, after all, require *speaking*. This means that in our disagreements, we must not only listen but also lean in and engage, with kindness and courage, as best we can. We must use our speech to help, to clarify, to convince, and to win over. Doing so is both strategic and Christ-like.

Jesus, give us the words that will bring your healing and blessing to those around us!

Discussion Questions

1. When you are in a disagreement, what strategies have you found effective for disarming the other person and helping your words get a hearing?

2. How can we tell the difference between effective diplomacy and untruthful flattery? In seeking to build bridges, when do we know if we have gone too far?

3. Describe a time in which an argument was used effectively without the receiving party feeling alienated or embarrassed. What made this effective?

CHAPTER FIVE

LOVE

As I write this paragraph, the Christian world has been rocked with various scandals and public disagreements. Sometimes it seems we bounce from one controversy to the next, and they all play out on social media before a watching world. Each week something new seems to surface. I won't even give examples since, by the time you read this, they will likely seem like ancient history! But sadly, as you read this paragraph, there will almost certainly be new disagreements that are producing more heat than light, alienating people and hardening them against each other, and doing nothing to advance the cause of Christ. If you are paying attention to the state of discourse in the body of Christ, you are probably well familiar with this troubling trend by now.

As we have emphasized throughout this book, disagreement *itself* is not the problem. But what grieves me these days is the way we *conduct* our disagreements: without any sense of love for one another. In the worst cases, we display the same rancor and "cancel culture" tactics of the world around us.

If I could change one thing about public Christian discourse, it would be this: that all our disagreements, however vigorous, would be constrained and beautified by those two great teachings of Jesus that we looked at in the introduction—his words in John 13 about love and in John 17 about unity:

> *A new commandment I give to you, that you love one another: just as I have loved you, you also are to love one another. **By this all people will know that you are my disciples**, if you have love for one another.*
>
> *(John 13:34-35)*

> *I do not ask for these only, but also for those who will believe in me through their word, that they may all be one, just as you, Father, are in me, and I in you, that they also may be in us, **so that the world may believe that you have sent me**. The glory that you have given me I have given to them, that they may be one even as we are one, I in them and you in me, that they may become perfectly one, **so that the world may know that you sent me and loved them even as you loved me**.*
>
> *(John 17:20-23)*

What stands out in both (note what I have emphasized) is that the world's perception of Jesus is affected by how Christians treat one another. Note, not by how we treat the *world*. No, Jesus is teaching that the way Christians treat *each other* will affect how the world responds to the gospel. And what Jesus calls us to is this: *love*.

Now, granted, working out what love looks like in different scenarios may be complicated. But the basic principle here is quite simple: when we love other Christians, we make the gospel more credible in the eyes of the world. When we fail to love other Christians, we put stumbling blocks in the paths of our friends considering the claims of Christianity.

The 20th-century theologian Francis Schaeffer spoke much of these chapters in John in calling for Christians to love each other. He termed Christian love the "final apologetic," emphasizing that Jesus gave the world the right to judge whether we are Christians by whether we live out the gospel's call to love each other.

One profoundly important way in which Christians love each other is in *how we disagree*. And friends, today we are largely failing at loving each other in our disagreements!

In disagreement, one way in which love manifests itself is by desiring to win the person more than the argument. Schaeffer wisely wrote:

"We all love to win. In fact, there is nobody who loves to win more than the theologian ... But we should understand that what we are working for in the midst of our differences is a solution—a solution that will give God the glory, that will be true to the Bible, but will exhibit the love of God simultaneously with his holiness. What is our attitude as we sit down to talk to our brother or as group meets with group to discuss differences? A desire to come out on top? To play one-upmanship? If there is any

*desire for love whatsoever, every time we discuss a
difference, we will desire a solution and not just that
we can be proven right."* [24]

In any disagreement, we must lay down any desire to
come out on top, to win, to look good. These concerns
must die at the foot of the cross. Instead, our ambition
should be to *honor the truth in love.* For some of us
(especially us hedgehogs), this means taking courage to
speak out. But for others (especially rhinos!), it means
remembering the priority of love. Truth without love is
not only insufficient but ugly.

The call to love means we must also lay aside any
agenda that has to do with our own reputation or ego
or selfish desires, and instead seek the broader good of
the kingdom of Christ. In every disagreement, we must
constantly ask, *What will be pleasing to Christ?* And also,
What will build up my brother or my sister?

Love is not easy or formulaic, and it does not mean the
absence of accountability or expression of concern. But
it does mean that we sincerely, with all our hearts, wish
others well, even amid our disagreements. It is through
love that we can find the healing of our divisions in
the church and find ways to move forward. "Above all,
keep loving one another earnestly, since love covers a
multitude of sins" (1 Peter 4:8).

Love is the essential key to everything else we've worked
through in this book. If we have sincere love for others,
all the other principles we have discussed will fall into

---

24 Francis Schaeffer, *The Mark of the Christian* (InterVarsity USA, 1970),
 p. 50.

place (and, when they don't, we'll be quick to recognize that and be ready to say sorry and ask for forgiveness). The art of disagreeing rests on the presence of real love. And this love must start in our hearts with a deep acceptance of what Christ has done for us on the cross. The more we appreciate the magnitude of what he has done for us—providing full forgiveness and new life—the more we can carry this love with us into our relationships with others, especially our fellow brothers and sisters in Christ.

Can you imagine how the church might be changed and the world might be impacted if we conducted our disagreements with the love of Christ? Isn't that worth recommitting ourselves to and prioritizing in everything else we do? Will you join me in seeking this afresh?

Picture once again that conversation at the Thanksgiving table. Disagreements arose, and it was uncomfortable. But each person also left the conversation feeling respected and sensing that the others around the table were ultimately for them, not against them. There was not agreement, but there was love. Don't we all want to see more of this?

I realize that not every disagreement will play out this way. There are some people we may need to simply avoid because they are unsafe. And there are some conversations we need to wait on. But as we look for opportunities to stretch forward in love toward those with whom we disagree, the Lord may open surprising doors. We may even find our holiday meals growing longer, and more interesting.

Jesus, fill our hearts to the brim until they overflow with love to others. No matter how vigorous our disagreements may be, may your love shine through so powerfully that the world may see that you are real. Amen.

Acknowledgments

Some of the ideas in this book germinated during a Wednesday-night series I taught at Immanuel Nashville. I'm thankful to have such a wonderful church community, whose feedback enriched this work in many ways. I'm grateful to everyone at The Good Book Company who helped improve this book, especially Carl Laferton for initially suggesting the idea and providing such insightful feedback on an early draft. Special thanks to my wife, Esther, whose wisdom has influenced so much of this book and whose support and friendship mean the world to me. I love chasing our dreams together.

COMPANY

BIBLICAL | RELEVANT | ACCESSIBLE

At The Good Book Company we are dedicated to helping Christians and local churches grow. We believe that God's growth process always starts with hearing clearly what he has said to us through his timeless and flawless word—the Bible.

Ever since we opened our doors in 1991, we have been striving to produce resources that are biblical, relevant, and accessible. By God's grace, we have grown to become an international publisher, encouraging ordinary Christians of every age and stage and every background and denomination to live for Christ day by day and equipping churches to grow in their knowledge of God, their love for one another, and the effectiveness of their outreach.

Call one of our friendly team for a discussion of your needs or visit one of our local websites for more information on the resources and services we provide.

Your friends at The Good Book Company

thegoodbook.com | thegoodbook.co.uk
thegoodbook.com.au | thegoodbook.co.nz
thegoodbook.co.in